Chocolate
the Bunny Rabbit

An Animal Discovery Book

Ruth C. Wiseman

Scribal Scion Science

In Loving Memory of
Jillian Leslie Hopewell

Chocolate the Bunny Rabbit

An Animal Discovery Book

Ruth C. Wiseman

For more information about Scribal Scion Publishing LLC, please visit:
https://scribalscionpublishing.com

ISBN-13: 9798886650228 (paperback)

Published by Scribal Scion Science

Scribal Scion Science is an imprint of Scribal Scion Publishing LLC, Teaneck NJ, USA

So much grass,
so little time.

Hi. My name is Chocolate.
I am a dark brown, short-haired rabbit.

Rabbits come in all colors and sizes.
Can you guess how I got my name?

Nope.

Munch, munch.

How?

Hey, Chocolate, got any chocolate?
Rabbits don't eat chocolate, silly!

I live in the school science room.
But if I lived in the wild, I would burrow
with my family in a meadow or in a forest.

Hellooo??? My lettuce is gone, people...

I am a vegan. My favorite foods are kale, lettuce, hay, and dandelions. I also love to have a treat of berries or bananas.

Let's have a race! On your mark, get set, GO!
I am so going to win.
Must. Clean. Foot.
Ooh, that smells good.
Hey, where's that turtle?
Slow and steady wins the race.

Vegetables keep me very healthy.
So healthy, in fact, that I run races
with my turtle friend.

I eat lots and lots of rough hay
to prevent my teeth from
growing too big for my mouth!

Chocolate eats hay instead of brushing her teeth.

Morris chews on twigs
and seeds for his teeth.

I am very, very soft. I keep my fur super clean.
My school friends love to hold me.

Time for my vitamins.

Well, the truth is
I need to stay clean because
I eat my poop. It's true.
I don't know why, but I do.

Wait!

There is something ELSE really cool about me.

I can swivel my ears 270 degrees.

I know where any sound is coming from.

I can see in every direction without turning my head, and I know when danger is near, even at night.

Time to hide!

I am not a hunter, just a cute bunny.
If another animal wants to catch me,
I protect myself by running very fast.

You got this, Chocolate!

Phew. I made it.

I am very good at hiding.
It is cozy in my burrow.

Rabbit
(Chocolate)

But I am safe here at school.
Come see me soon!

Fun Facts About Bunny Rabbits

There are over 300 breeds of domestic rabbits worldwide.

Baby rabbits are called kits or kittens.

Rabbits live in deserts, forests, meadows, and even some cities!

Rabbits should never be given processed human foods to eat, like bread, cookies, or yogurt.

85% of a rabbit's diet consists of hay.

Rabbit teeth do not stop growing. Hay creates enough friction, like sandpaper, to "file" their teeth. The grinding motion of their jaws while chewing hay also wears down their teeth.

Rabbits grow extra fur during the winter to keep them warm.

Rabbits (and mice) eat their poop at night. This is called cecotrophy: it increases Vitamin B-12 and folic acid intake. Most pet rabbits already have these nutrients in their diet and do this out of instinct.

Rabbits have almost 360 degree vision, as well as excellent night vision, to better detect danger. But they cannot see straight ahead!

Rabbits sleep between 8 to 12 hours a day…. so should you!

About the Author

Ruth C. Wiseman is an author and illustrator of children's picture books. Ruth writes first drafts with pen on paper, enjoying the tactile feel and sound of the pen as it moves on paper. Ruth's sixth grade public school teacher encouraged her in her writing. His kind words and earnest support stayed with her all her life. It showed her how a child's positive relationship with an adult in their life, however brief, can have a very strong and lasting impact.

Ruth wrote the children's picture book *How the Moon Became Dim* (2017), and wrote and illustrated *Melech the Bearded Dragon* (2025), the first of a series of children's science picture books about animals for children ages 5 to 8. *Chocolate the Bunny Rabbit* is her second book in the series.

Ruth loves to rescue cats, small dogs, crested geckos, and books. Her favorite pastimes are being in nature, drinking a good cup of strong tea, writing in a quiet place, and reading a suspenseful adventure story. Perfection is when all of those things happen on the same day.